From Me to You!

Gifted TO:

Gifted FROM:

DATE:

A Hair Journal
—— *for the* ——
Curly, Kinky & Coily

LAYLA BRYANT

PEN WILD

Published and Printed in the U.S.A. by
Pen Wild, LLC
Atlanta, GA U.S.A.

Naturally You © 2016 by Tauheedah Rashid
All rights reserved.

No part of this book may be reproduced in any written, electronic, recording, or photocopying form without prior written permission of the copyright holder.

For information about special discounts for bulk purchases or custom editions, please email info@penwild.com.

Illustrated by Philece R.
Designed by Brian Hodge

ISBN: 978-0-692-48058-8

10 9 8 7 6 5 4 3 2 1

Dedicated to my ZoZo B
and her gorgeous strands of natural and free.

From One Naturalista to Another...

What exactly does it mean to be natural? Are we going natural or are we returning to natural? Are the bloggers and vloggers and books giving us the right information on how to care for our natural hair? Or is the flood of conflicting opinions overwhelming? Is the concept of "good hair" a thing of the past? Or has the search for the perfect curl given it new life?

These are but a few of the many questions being discussed within the natural hair community. And there are as many answers as there are naturalistas. Our journey is a deliberate one and along the path we find self-discovery, candid conversation, and kindred spirits. In all of the passion, pride, struggle, and debate, one thing is quite clear: being natural is more than just a beauty statement.

I decided to go natural for one reason alone — relaxers were burning my scalp. In spite of the preparation and precautions I took before and after getting a perm, I still managed to find several damaged spots with scabs. The day I decided I'd had enough was my first big chop. That was over fifteen years ago and since that time, I've found many reasons to stay natural.

Every woman has a personal story about going and/or being natural. The Naturally You journal is an opportunity to define what being natural means to you. There are no right or wrong answers. Each question is designed to help you express how natural hair plays a part in how you view yourself and interact with the world.

Some questions are best answered with the first thought that comes to mind, while others are better served by some contemplation. Although some questions are prompted with yes/no or true/false, space is given to elaborate on your responses. You may choose to write your thoughts privately or share with a circle of friends. Either way you will get the most out of this experience by being true to your own natural hair journey. In this space it is my hope that you will uncover in a fun and engaging way your own criteria for being *Naturally You*.

–Layla Bryant

Contents

Glorious Me
11

My Crown
13

My Hairstory
15

The Great Migration
21

In My City
29

Daily Do
35

Hair Healthy
43

Mane Attraction
55

Product Junkie
59

Curly Demographics
67

Salon Trip
73

A Month in the Life of a Naturalista
79

Hair Esteem
81

Curlosophy
89

The Long and Short of It
97

Curl Connection
101

Media Frizz
109

Blogs, Vlogs and Posts, Oh My!
113

The Hall of Mane Fame
119

Hair Innovation
123

Natural Hair Glossary
129

Free Style Flow aka Notes
133

Acknowledgements
141

Glorious Me

Name:

Nickname:

Actual age: *Age you feel:*

Ethnicity:

Hometown:

City of residence:

Current 9 to 5:

Dream occupation:

Affiliations (sorority, associations, organizations, faith-based):

Favorite place in the world:

Single or in a relationship?

straight —————————— ①

wavy ～～～～～ ② abc

curly ℓℓℓℓℓ ③ abc

kinky ∧∨∧∨∧∨∧∨ ④ abc

My Crown

I have been natural since:

I classify my natural hair texture as type: (Circle one)
(**1, 2A, 2B, 2C, 3A, 3B, 3C, 4A, 4B, 4C, *I have no idea*)**

I have multiple textures on my head: ○ Yes ○ No

Hair density: ○ Thick ○ Medium ○ Fine

Natural hair color:

Current hair color:

Hair length:
- ○ Caesar
- ○ TWA
- ○ Chin Length
- ○ Shoulder Length
- ○ Bra Strap
- ○ Beyond Bra Strap

My primary hair goals are to: (check all that apply)
- ○ Increase length
- ○ Add fullness
- ○ Repair damaged hair
- ○ Lock in moisture
- ○ Learn better styling
- ○ Other:

My Hairstory

The hair products we used growing up were:

What I remember about my mother's hair:

The person who combed my hair most often was:

MY HAIRSTORY

Looking back on school pictures from my early years, I think to myself:
- ○ *I totally rocked that style!*
- ○ *Well...it was popular at the time.*
- ○ *Who let me leave the house this way?*
- ○ *Other:*

As a young girl, I was teased about my hair: ○ *Yes* ○ *No*

I styled my siblings' hair: ○ *Yes* ○ *No*

I've always been natural: ○ *Yes* ○ *No*

I wasn't allowed to relax my hair as a child because:

I wish I was allowed to get a perm as a youth: ○ *Yes* ○ *No*

It was hard growing up natural because:

I received my first relaxer at age:

MY HAIRSTORY

The person who gave me my first perm:

I used a home relaxer kit called:

I prepared for getting a perm by:
- ○ *Not combing my hair for a day.*
- ○ *Applying petroleum jelly to my scalp and edges.*
- ○ *Dividing my hair into small sections.*
- ○ *All of the above*
- ○ *Other:*

Having straightened hair made me feel:

My happiest hair memory is:

MY HAIRSTORY

My first hair catastrophe was:

....

....

....

....

....

....

I remember the smell of:
- ○ *The relaxer we used.*
- ○ *Our hair grease.*
- ○ *A press and curl.*
- ○ *All of the above.*
- ○ *Other:*

....

....

I remember the feel of:
- ○ *My mother combing my hair.*
- ○ *The hot comb on my scalp.*
- ○ *Getting cornrows.*
- ○ *All of the above*
- ○ *Other:*

....

MY HAIRSTORY

I remember the sound of:

- ○ *The hot comb and grease sizzle.*
- ○ *The brush running along my tresses.*
- ○ *Beads shaking on my braids.*
- ○ *All of the above.*
- ○ *Other:*

....

....

....

My first visit to the hair salon was:
....

....

....

....

I had complete autonomy over my hair at age:
....

....

....

....

....

....

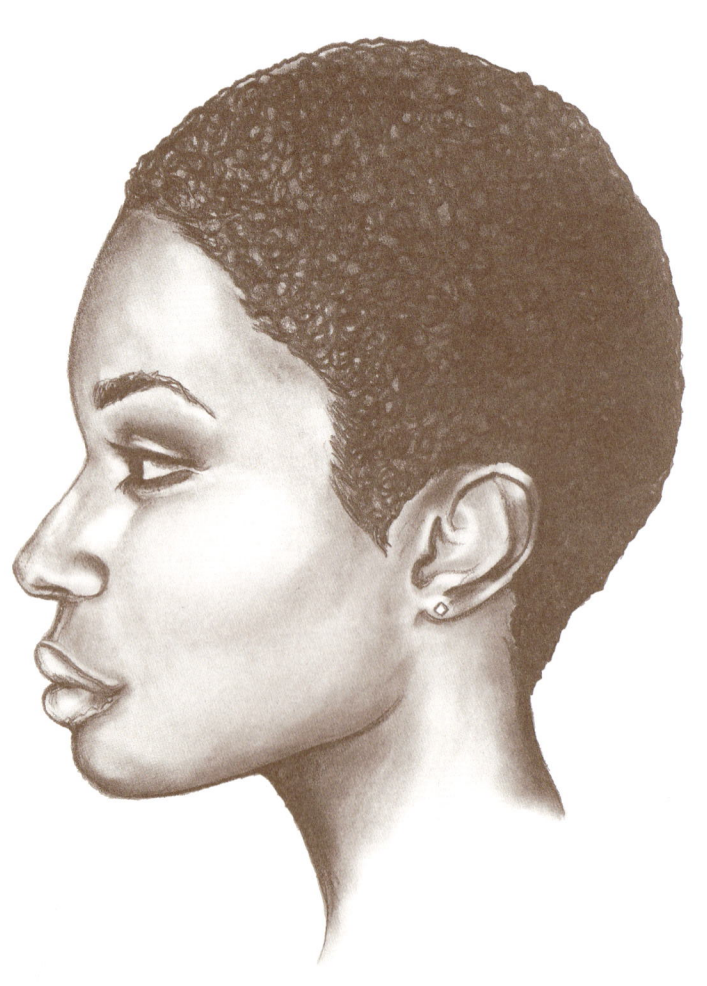

The Great Migration

I researched ways to go natural: ○ Yes or ○ No

When researching going natural I felt:
- ○ Informed
- ○ Overwhelmed

Deciding to go natural was:
- ○ A big decision
- ○ No big deal

After I decided to go natural I was:
- ○ Excited
- ○ Tentative
- ○ Indifferent

I have relapsed into processed hair _____ times.

What I miss most about having processed/relaxed hair is:

What I miss least about having processed/relaxed hair is:

The person who influenced me to go natural:

The first person I told I was going natural:

The person who tried to tried to talk me out of going natural:

THE GREAT MIGRATION

I am still natural in this moment because:

I went natural with a Big Chop (BC): ○ Yes or ○ No

I decided to do a BC because:

The date I did my first BC:

My BC was done by a professional: ○ Yes or ○ No

The person who cut my hair was:

After my first BC, I:
- ○ Cried tears of joy
- ○ Cried tears of sorrow
- ○ Kept it moving

THE GREAT MIGRATION

After my first BC, I looked:

The first person to see me after my BC was:

His or her reaction was:

The length of my hair after my first BC:

After my BC I tended to wear more:
- ○ Makeup
- ○ Dressy clothes
- ○ Accessories
- ○ All of the above
- ○ None of the above

A teeny weeny afro (TWA) looks great on me: ○ Yes or ○ No

THE GREAT MIGRATION

My favorite post-BC products and tools are:

I have done a BC _____ times.

A BC is easier than transitioning. ○ *True* or ○ *False*

I would recommend a BC over transitioning to a friend: ○ *Yes* or ○ *No*

I went natural by transitioning out of processed hair: ○ *Yes* or ○ *No*

I decided to transition into a natural state because:

The date I started transitioning:

A professional assisted me with the transitioning process: ○ *Yes* or ○ *No*

My favorite products for transitioning hair are:

My favorite tools for transitioning hair are:

My favorite styles for transitioning hair are:

THE GREAT MIGRATION

I trimmed my hair every .... while transitioning.

Transitioning is easier than a BC.   ○ *True* or ○ *False*

I would recommend transitioning over a BC to a friend: ○ *Yes* or ○ *No*

If I were beginning my natural hair journey again I would:

In My City

Find in your city or region...

Natural stylists for Cuts

Natural stylists for Color

IN MY CITY

Natural stylists for Styles

Natural stylists for Growth and maintenance

IN MY CITY

Natural hair meet ups

Places to buy natural hair care products

Places to buy hair accessories

IN MY CITY

Natural hair shows dates and locations

Natural hair workshop or styling classes

IN MY CITY

5 local natural friends with whom you
can share your natural hair journey:

Friend 1

Friend 2

Friend 3

Friend 4

Friend 5

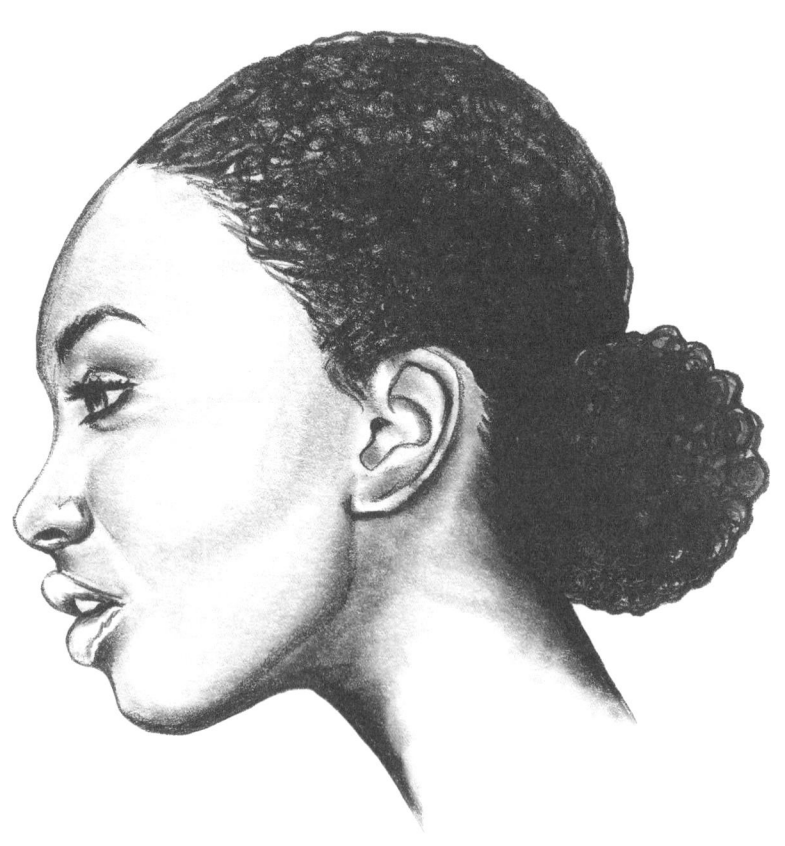

Daily Do

*I am a **beginner, intermediate, expert** at doing my own hair. (Circle One)*

The average amount of time I spend on my hair daily:

My styling speed on a scale of 1 – 10:

I try to achieve hair perfection daily: ○ Yes or ○ No

I am an efficient stylist and can hit the right look in 1 or 2 attempts: ○ Yes or ○ No

It takes several rounds and tweaking to get the look I want each day: ○ Yes or ○ No

I use a hand mirror while styling to clearly see the back of my head: ○ Yes or ○ No

My go-to style on a bad hair day:

DAILY DO

The style I've worn too long is:

Hairstyles that look better on me as I mature:

I was around when the afro was popular in the 60's/70's: ○ Yes or ○ No

I dye my hair: ○ Yes or ○ No

    a) If yes, what color?

    b) If no, why not?

If I weren't so afraid, I would try the following style:

DAILY DO

I change my hair style every:

I would never wear my hair:

One day, I would like to try my hair in this style:

The best time to try a new hair style is:

A style that looks completely different at the end of the day than it does at the beginning:

A style that looks just as good at the end of the day as it does at the beginning:

DAILY DO

The best daily solution for your hair (Circle one):

○ *Single product:*

○ *Combination of several products:*

Shrinkage is the enemy of natural hair styling: ○ Yes or ○ No

How the climate affects my hair:

Hair products/tools I carry in my purse:

DAILY DO

Hair and outfits are meant to coordinate: ○ True or ○ False

....

I love to accessorize and adorn my hair: ○ Yes or ○ No

I am diligent in keeping up my nighttime maintenance routine: ○ Yes or ○ No

My nighttime routine includes (check all that apply):	○ Adding an oil or cream
	○ Combing and/or brushing
	○ Protective styling – twists, braids, etc.
	○ Pinning hair
	○ Rollers
	○ Tying down hair
	○ Other:

My hairstyling soundtrack includes these favorite songs:

....

....

....

....

....

Sense of Styling

Are you a style adventurer? Which styles have you completed on yourself and/or a friend? Circle the (✓) for YES and the (✗) for NO.

Style	Completed on myself		Completed on someone else	
Cornrows	✓	✗	✓	✗
Flat Twists	✓	✗	✓	✗
Bantu Knots	✓	✗	✓	✗
Twist Out	✓	✗	✓	✗
Sisterlocks	✓	✗	✓	✗
Wash and Go	✓	✗	✓	✗
Locs	✓	✗	✓	✗
Box Braids	✓	✗	✓	✗
Comb Coils	✓	✗	✓	✗
Crochet Braids	✓	✗	✓	✗

Sense of Styling

Include additional styles you've tried below.

Style	Completed on myself		Completed on someone else	
	✓	✗	✓	✗
	✓	✗	✓	✗
	✓	✗	✓	✗
	✓	✗	✓	✗
	✓	✗	✓	✗
	✓	✗	✓	✗
	✓	✗	✓	✗
	✓	✗	✓	✗
	✓	✗	✓	✗
	✓	✗	✓	✗

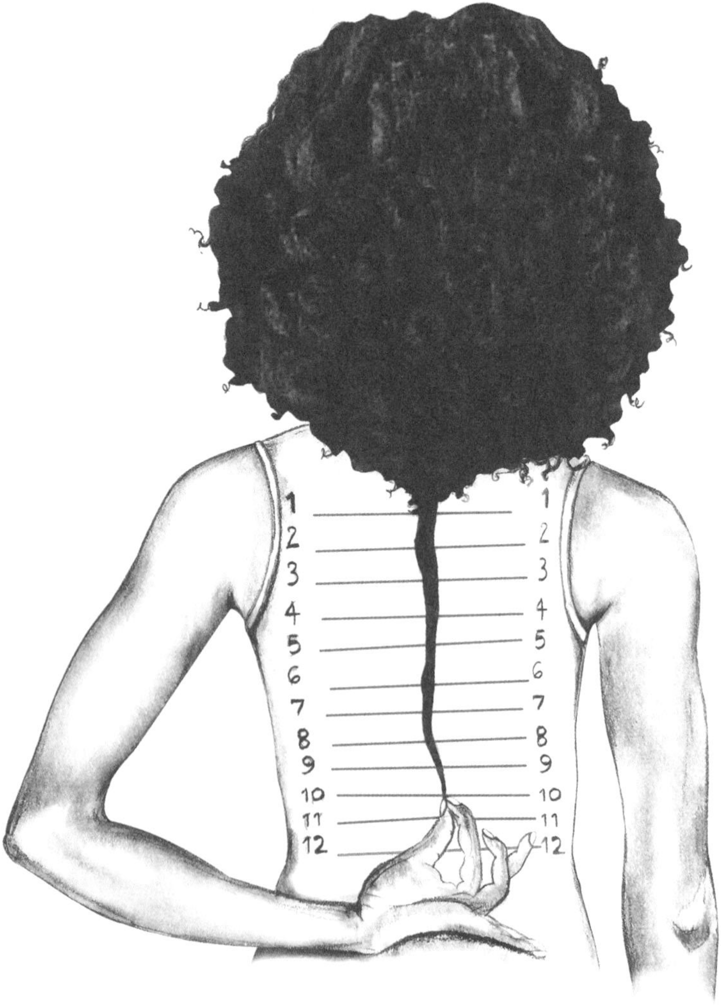
1
2
3
4
5
6
7
8
9
10
11
12
1
2
3
4
5
6
7
8
9
10
11
12

Hair Healthy

My hair is healthy right now. ○ Yes or ○ No

I struggle with dry hair and/or scalp: ○ Yes or ○ No

The hands-down best deep-conditioning technique:

Wetting natural hair daily is:

The best products for keeping my hair healthy are:

I never use the following products on my hair:

HAIR HEALTHY

I am interested in the science behind hair: ○ *Yes or* ○ *No*

I review the ingredient list before purchasing a product: ○ *Yes or* ○ *No*

I understand what most of the ingredients are in a product and what they do: ○ *Yes or* ○ *No*

I know what ingredients are considered unhealthy: ○ *Yes or* ○ *No*

Using organic products is important to me: ○ *Yes or* ○ *No*

I understand how products impact the environment: ○ *Yes or* ○ *No*

Chemicals from processing products penetrate the scalp: ○ *True or* ○ *False*

I groom my hair using the following tools:

HAIR HEALTHY

I never use the following tools on my hair:

I lost my curl pattern using the following process, product, or tool(s):

I regularly use heat to straighten my hair: ○ Yes or ○ No

My thoughts on heat styling are:

Hair growth has been a challenge for me: ○ Yes or ○ No

There are products that can enhance hair growth: ○ True or ○ False

A significant portion of my hair fell out when:

If I ever lost all of my hair, I would:

HAIR HEALTHY

I would cut off all my hair for the following cause:

Over the years, my hair has become:

Having natural hair has influenced my overall awareness of being healthy: ○ *Yes* or ○ *No*

HAIR HEALTHY

How working out affects my natural hair:

My scalp sweats easily during physical activity: ○ Yes or ○ No

I sometimes skip exercise because of what it does to my hair: ○ True or ○ False

How pregnancy affects my hair:

What we eat affects the health of our hair: ○ True or ○ False

I take vitamins specifically to strengthen my hair: ○ Yes or ○ No

Getting Kinky in the Kitchen

Product Name:

Product Purpose:

        Amount   Ingredient

List the recipe of a product you created from scratch.

Instructions

Getting Kinky in the Kitchen

Product Name:

Product Purpose:

          Amount   *Ingredient*

List the recipe of a product you created from scratch.

Instructions

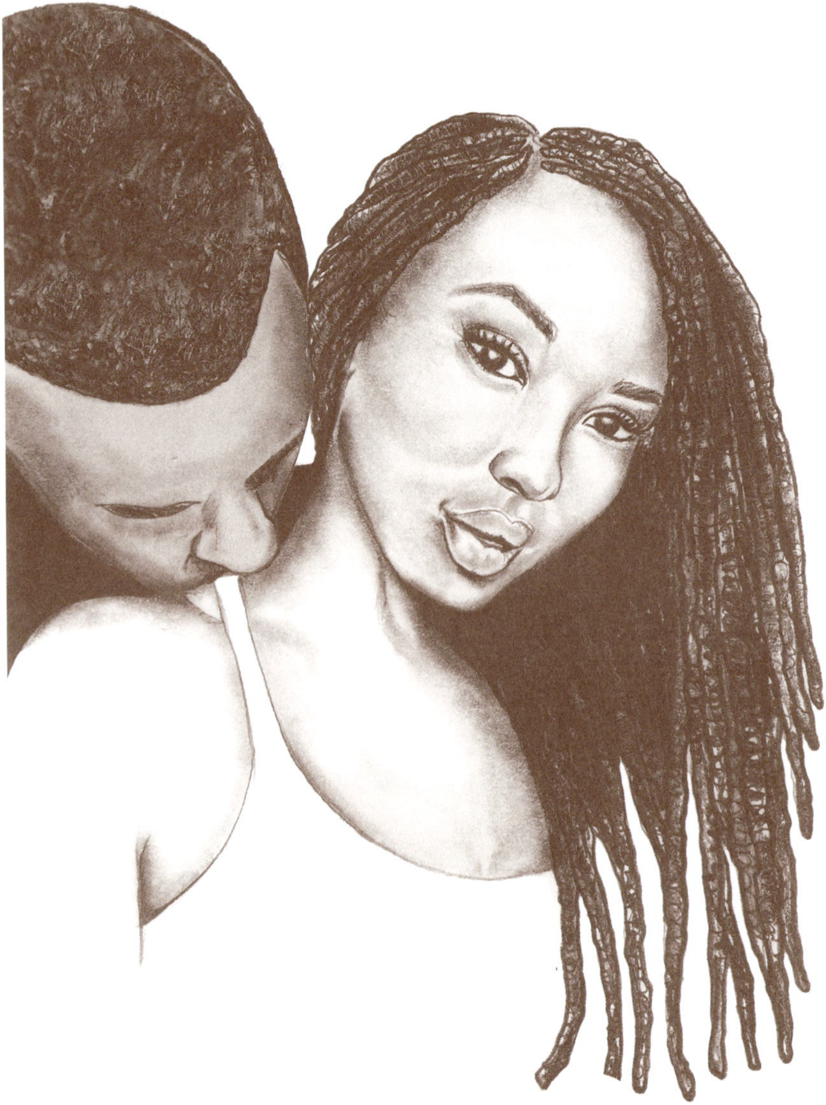

Mane Attraction

I feel sexy when my hair:

A style I find particularly seductive:

The first time my significant other saw my natural hair:

MANE ATTRACTION

My significant other ○ Loves / ○ Hates / ○ Tolerates my natural hair:

*My significant other **always / never** touches my hair. (Circle One)*

My hair/scalp is an erogenous zone: ○ Yes or ○ No

When being intimate most people don't give the hair/scalp enough attention: ○ True or ○ False

Pulling my hair while being intimate:
- ○ Drives me wild…in a good way.
- ○ Makes me want to slap someone… not in a good way.
- ○ Is too dramatic and only done in the movies.

It really turns me on when someone does this to my hair:

It really turns me off when someone does this to my hair:

Longer hair is more attractive: ○ True or ○ False

MANE ATTRACTION

A softer/smoother texture of hair is more attractive: ○ True or ○ False

I flirt using my hair: ○ Yes or ○ No

My favorite hairstyle for a date:

I love the fragrance of _____ *in hair.*

The fragrance of my hair is:

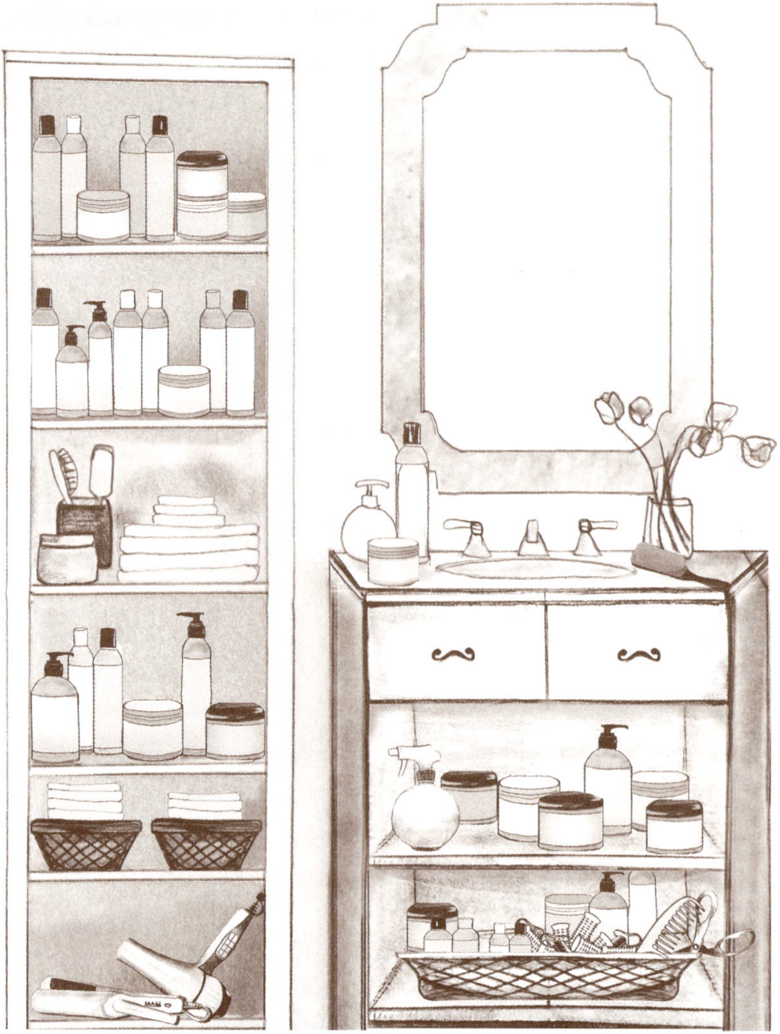

Product Junkie

Hello, my name is .... *and I am a product junkie.*

I pride myself on using as few products in my hair as possible: ○ *Yes* or ○ *No*

The perfect product will do the following for my hair:

....

....

....

The number of reviews I look at before trying new products:

....

Most of my reviews come from:	○ *Magazines*
	○ *Blogs*
	○ *Vlogs*
	○ *People I know*

PRODUCT JUNKIE

I decide to purchase a product based on the following criteria:

What the packaging and shelf presentation tell me about a product:

The length of time I try a product before I decide to add it to my routine:

What I do with products that don't work for me:

The number of products that are a part of my routine at any given time:

I use several products in a single brand or individual products across a variety of brands: ○ Yes or ○ No

PRODUCT JUNKIE

It is important to have more than one kind of the same product, i.e. multiple shampoos: ○ True or ○ False

Why?

The product(s) I have used the longest:

The product or brand I knew wasn't for me after one use:

Products I buy just for the scent:

The brand(s) I use the most:

PRODUCT JUNKIE

What happens more often: you asking for product recommendations or being asked for product recommendations?

The product(s) I recommend the most:

If I were to create a line of hair products, I would name it:

I have products located in the following areas of my home (check all that apply).
- ○ Bathroom
- ○ Bedroom
- ○ Kitchen
- ○ Pantry
- ○ Closet
- ○ Other

My favorite location(s) to buy products:

I have a monthly budget for my hair care: ○ Yes or ○ No

PRODUCT JUNKIE

I spend about $ _____ on my hair regimen each month.

*When I had a relaxer, I spent **more, less,** or **about the same** on my hair each month. (Circle One)*

The hair product that is the best bargain:

The hair product that is worth every penny:

The hair product I only buy when it's on sale:

I often spend money on products I never end up finishing: ○ Yes or ○ No

I believe there is a set of products out there so perfect for my hair that one day I won't have to look any longer: ○ Yes or ○ No

Bathroom Raid!

List everything you have in your bathroom right now related to hair—consider what you like, don't like about them, and the results achieved on your hair, then rate them from 1 to 5, with 1 being "Toss It!" and 5 being "Must Have."

Product/Tool	Rating	Notes
	1 2 3 4 5	
	1 2 3 4 5	
	1 2 3 4 5	
	1 2 3 4 5	
	1 2 3 4 5	
	1 2 3 4 5	

Bathroom Raid!

List everything you have in your bathroom right now related to hair—consider what you like, don't like about them, and the results achieved on your hair, then rate them from 1 to 5, with 1 being "Toss It!" and 5 being "Must Have."

Product/Tool	Rating	Notes
	1 2 3 4 5	
	1 2 3 4 5	
	1 2 3 4 5	
	1 2 3 4 5	
	1 2 3 4 5	
	1 2 3 4 5	

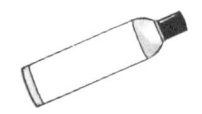

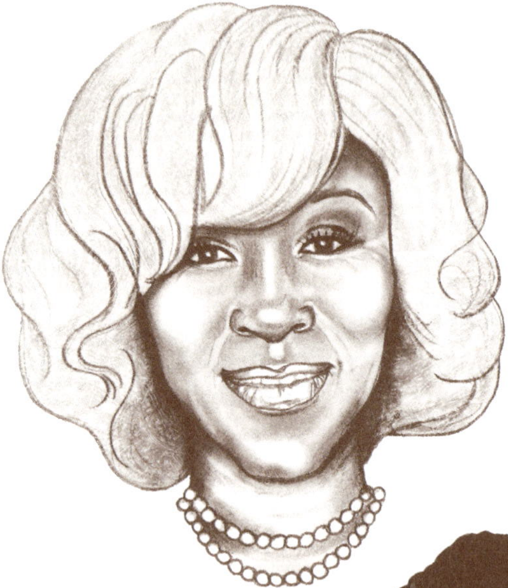

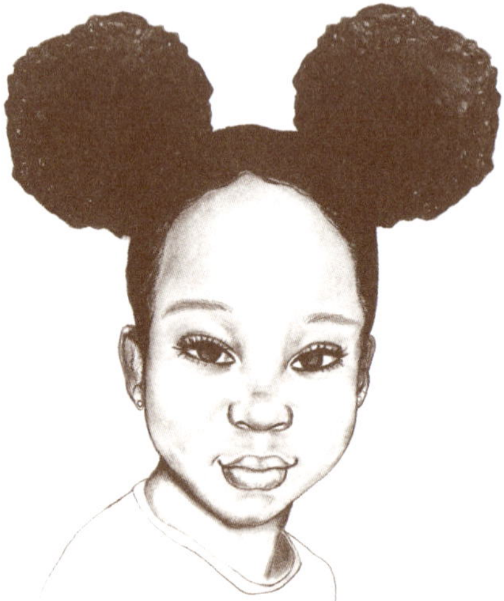

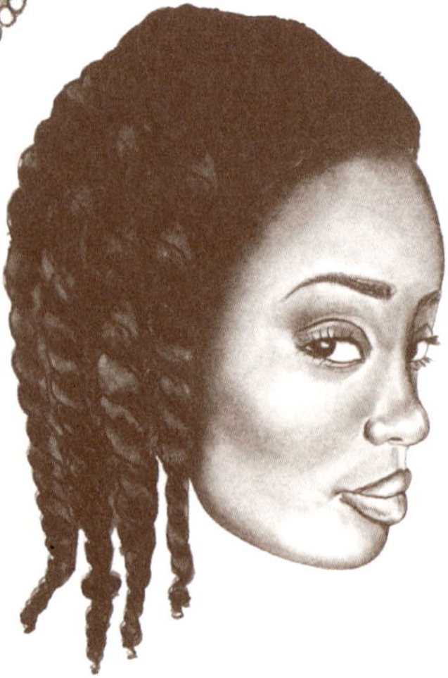

Curly Demographics

Is "Natural" the best term to describe natural hair: ○ Yes or ○ No

What is the best term to describe women with natural hair:

Can someone be more natural than another: ○ Yes or ○ No

How or why not?

CURLY DEMOGRAPHICS

The natural hair community is exclusive to women: ○ *True* or ○ *False*

Hair typing is the best way to classify hair.   ○ *True* or ○ *False*

I understand the concept of hair typing and how it came about: ○ *Yes* or ○ *No*

It is easy to determine hair type.   ○ *True* or ○ *False*

Is it necessary to classify hair?   ○ *Yes* or ○ *No*

Mature women are well represented in the natural hair community: ○ *True* or ○ *False*

CURLY DEMOGRAPHICS

Young people are well represented in the natural hair community: ○ True or ○ False

Attitudes about hair differ by location: ○ True or ○ False

Natural hair is fairly common where I live: ○ Yes or ○ No

When it comes to the natural hair community I relate more to those who share my:
- ○ Ethnicity
- ○ Hair type
- ○ Hair style
- ○ Something else:

Natural is exclusive to particular ethnic group(s): ○ True or ○ False

How does being natural differ among various ethnicities and cultures?

CURLY DEMOGRAPHICS

I can learn about my hair from people with different hair types than my own: ○ *True or* ○ *False*

Describe your 3 closest friends:

Friend #1:

    a) Natural or Processed Hair

    b) Hair Type:

    c) General styling: **conservative** *or* **adventurous**

    d) Ethnicity: *e) Gender:*

    f) Age: *g) Hair Length:*

Friend #2:

    a) Natural or Processed Hair

    b) Hair Type:

    c) General styling: **conservative** *or* **adventurous**

    d) Ethnicity: *e) Gender:*

    f) Age: *g) Hair Length:*

Friend #3:

    a) Natural or Processed Hair

    b) Hair Type:

    c) General styling: **conservative** *or* **adventurous**

    d) Ethnicity: *e) Gender:*

    f) Age: *g) Hair Length:*

What do these 3 friends have in common:

How are these 3 friends different:

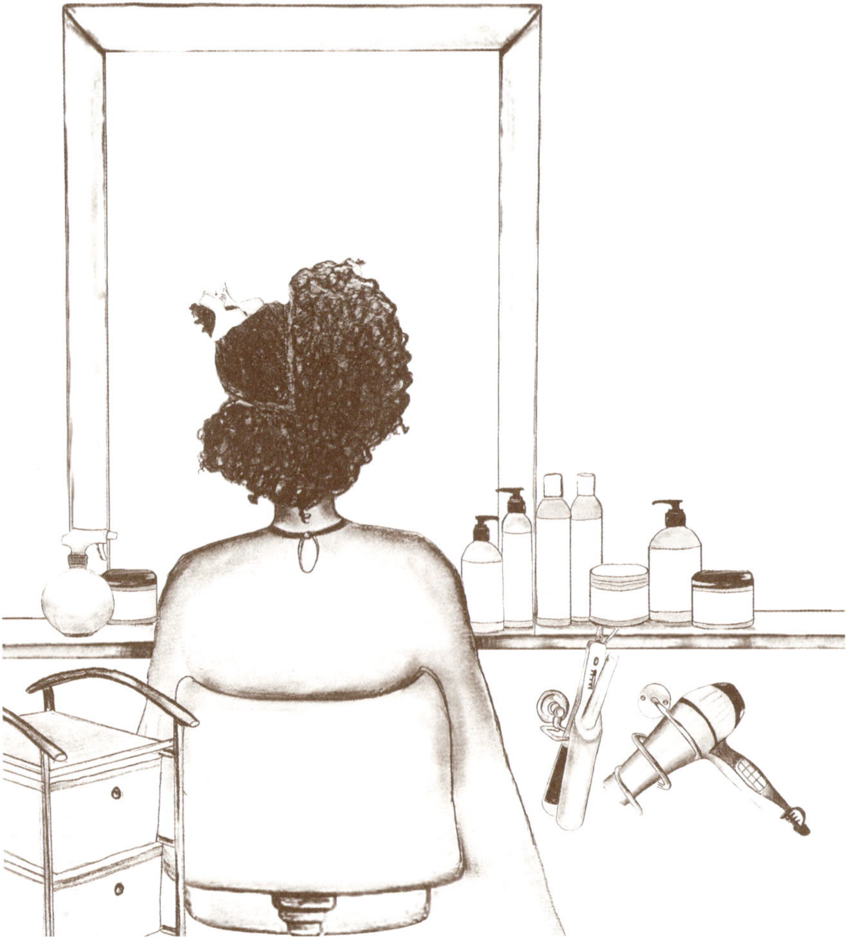

Salon Trip

There are plenty of natural hair stylists in my city: ○ True or ○ False

I enjoy going to the salon: ○ Yes or ○ No

A visit to the salon should be:
- ○ Efficient, like a well-run assembly line.
- ○ Relaxing, like a day at the spa.
- ○ Other:

Best experience at a salon with my natural hair:

SALON TRIP

Worst experience at a salon with my natural hair:

Being professionally styled is worth the time: ○ True or ○ False

Being professionally styled is worth the cost: ○ True or ○ False

The most I've ever paid to get my hair cut and/or styled:

Average length of time I spend at a salon visit:

SALON TRIP

It is common to receive a consultation prior to getting my natural hair done in a salon: ○ *Yes* or ○ *No*

Stylists are properly trained to work with natural hair: ○ *Yes* or ○ *No*

My hair is maintained by a barber: ○ *Yes* or ○ *No*

I prefer to have my hair done in a private space: ○ *Yes* or ○ *No*

I know my stylist well enough to:
- ○ *Give a wave if I pass them on the street.*
- ○ *Exchange pleasantries if I see them outside of the salon.*
- ○ *Invite them to a private event at my home.*

My stylist:
- ○ *Gives me exactly what I ask for.*
- ○ *Does what he/she thinks is best.*
- ○ *Helps me choose a style that is most flattering.*

I love my hair just as it is when I walk out of the salon: ○ *Yes* or ○ *No*

I put on a hat, scarf, or pull back in a ponytail when I leave the salon: ○ *Yes* or ○ *No*

I feel comfortable trying different stylists at the same salon: ○ *True* or ○ *False*

SALON TRIP

What can be done to improve the experiences I've had with natural hair professionals thus far:

I have thought about becoming a natural hair stylist: ○ Yes or ○ No

I have considered opening my own natural hair salon: ○ Yes or ○ No

The perfect name for a natural hair salon would be:

Salon Trip: Sketch Pad

Describe and design your ideal natural hair salon.

S	M	T	W	Th	F	S
	1	2	3	4	5	6
7	8	9	10	11	12	13
14	15	16	17	18	19	20
21	22	23	24	25	26	27
28	29	30				

A Month in the Life of a Naturalista

When do you:

Wash:

Moisturize:

Clarify:

Color:

Condition:

Take Vitamins:

Deep Condition:

Style Set:

Trim:

Visit Salon:

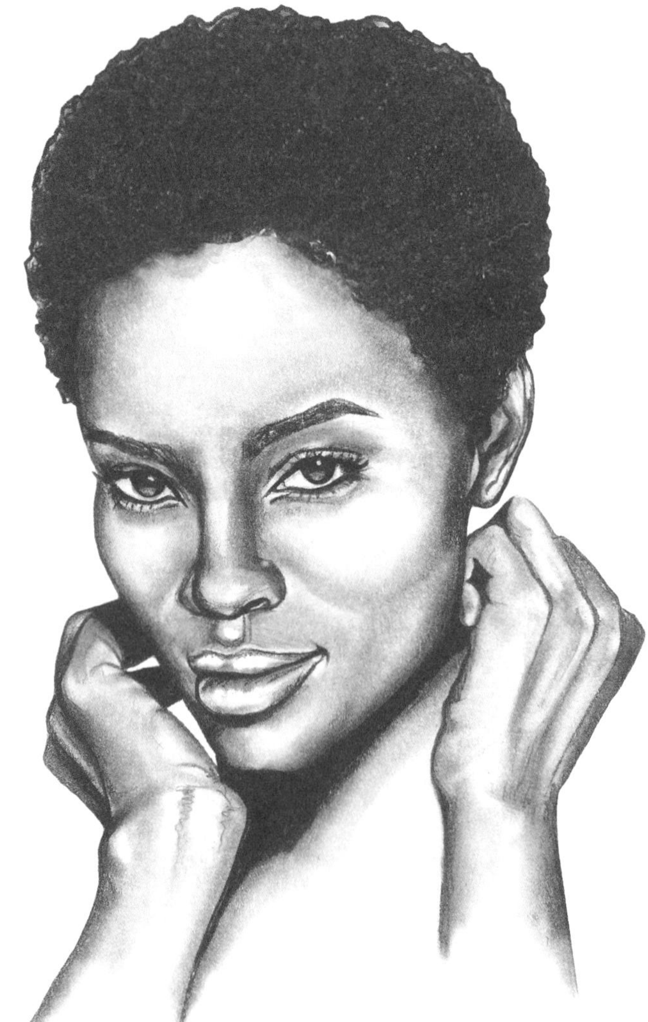

Hair Esteem

The moment I fell in love with my natural hair:

Hair should make you feel:

In this moment I feel _____ *about my hair.*

Hair influences self-esteem: ○ *True* or ○ *False*

Since going natural my self-esteem has:

HAIR ESTEEM

I feel self-conscious being natural: (Check all that apply)

- ○ At work
- ○ At school
- ○ In the bedroom
- ○ At a formal event
- ○ All of the above
- ○ Other:

I could walk the red carpet when my hair is:

I love my: (Check all that apply)

- ○ Edges
- ○ Crown
- ○ Curl pattern
- ○ Length
- ○ Hair type/Texture
- ○ Natural Color
- ○ Head shape
- ○ Overall natural look
- ○ Other:

A bad hair day is:

At its fiercest, my hair resembles the following animal:

HAIR ESTEEM

My hair is important to my overall look: ○ Yes or ○ No

Hair is more important than what I am wearing: ○ Yes or ○ No

I fix or adjust my hair multiple times a day: ○ Yes or ○ No

I once cried because the following happened to my hair:

I have seen my first gray hair: ○ Yes or ○ No

  If yes, I saw my first gray hair at the age of:

To gray hair, I say:
- ○ *Come back another day.*
- ○ *Bring it on, I'll rock that too!*
- ○ *Other:*

Seeing a fly natural on another woman makes me feel:
- ○ *Inspired*
- ○ *Jealous*
- ○ *Other:*

The last compliment I gave a person about their natural hair was:

HAIR ESTEEM

The best compliment I have ever received about my natural hair was:

The worse insult I ever received about my natural hair was:

I responded by:

I receive a lot of support related to being natural: ○ Yes or ○ No

I spend too much time thinking, reading, studying and watching videos about hair: ○ Yes or ○ No

I can spend hours playing with, analyzing, practicing new styles with my hair: ○ Yes or ○ No

Is there a hierarchy of beauty in the natural hair world?

What is it?

HAIR ESTEEM

I truly believe that all hair types are equally beautiful: ○ Yes or ○ No

I have done the following to my hair for emotional reasons:

I will never do the following to my hair again:

The perfect curl is achievable: ○ True or ○ False

I'm obsessed with achieving the perfect curl: ○ Yes or ○ No

Top 3 words that come to mind when I think of natural hair:

  #1:

  #2:

  #3:

Good hair is:

HAIR ESTEEM

Nappy hair is:

Kinky hair is:

Curly hair is:

Coily hair is:

I have_____hair:
(Check all that apply)
- ○ Good
- ○ Kinky
- ○ Curly
- ○ Coily
- ○ Nappy
- ○ Other:

A natural hair affirmation worth repeating every day:

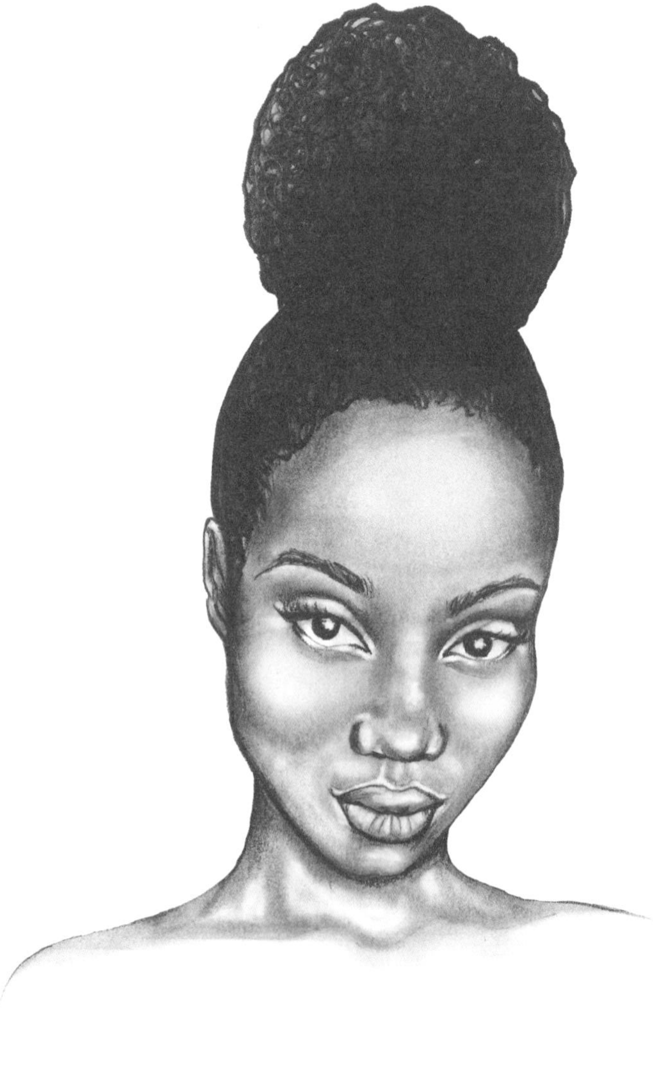

Curlosophy

"Un"natural hair is:

....

....

....

....

....

....

....

I believe everyone should wear their natural hair: ○ *Yes or* ○ *No*

My hair is a: ○ *Style preference*
○ *Political statement*
○ *Other:*

....

The worse thing a person can do to their hair is:

Wearing weaves is:

Wearing wigs is:

% of my friends wear their hair natural.

My best friend's hair is:

CURLOSOPHY

*My child(ren) will be allowed to make decisions
about their own hair at the age of:*

....

....

....

....

*My child(ren) will be allowed to
have processed hair if they want:* ○ Yes or ○ No

Natural hair is just another trend or fad: ○ True or ○ False

....

*The natural hair movement has caused a
divide in the community:* ○ True or ○ False

....

The natural hair community has put too much emphasis on:

....

....

*Achieving the perfect texture or curl has
become too important in the natural hair community.* ○ True or ○ False

....

....

CURLOSOPHY

I am offended by the word _____ *as it relates to natural hair.*

All natural styles are appropriate for the workplace: ○ True or ○ False

It is important to choose products and tools that are produced/owned by persons with a similar racial and cultural background as my own: ○ Yes or ○ No

If yes, why?

The state of my hair is dictated by my faith: ○ Yes or ○ No

CURLOSOPHY

I usually cover my hair: ○ Yes or ○ No

If yes, I cover my hair because:

*It **does / does not** matter what I do under my head garment. (Circle one)*

Under my head wrap, I style my hair: ○ Yes or ○ No

I allow a small bit of hair to show outside my head wrap: ○ Yes or ○ No

I only uncover my hair when:

The challenge of covered hair is:

The beauty of covered hair is:

CURLOSOPHY

A bias I have about natural hair that may not be true:

....

....

....

Going natural has affected other areas of my life, namely:

....

....

....

Going natural has made me more:

....

....

....

Going natural has made me less:

....

....

....

How much would someone have to pay you to process your natural hair?

....

....

My hair motto is: ○ *Go big or stay home.*
　　　　　　　　　　○ *Less is more.*
　　　　　　　　　　○ *Other:*

....

My hair tells the world that:

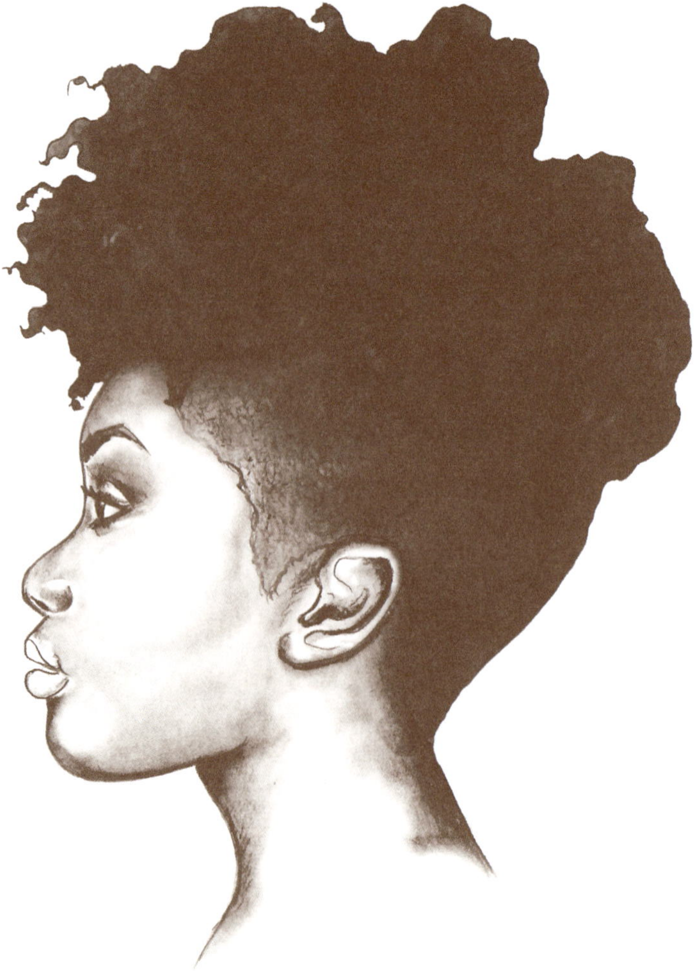

The Long and Short of It

Which do you favor? Circle one.

Brush | Comb

Shampoo | Co-wash

The old me | The new me

Touch my hair | Lose a limb

Everyone natural | Pro-choice

Locked | Loose

THE LONG AND SHORT OF IT

Tamed Locks | Grow as they may

I'd do it all over again | I should have kept my relaxer

Straight to the Big Chop | Slow transition

Blog | Vlog

TWA | Fro fabulous

DIY | Professional stylist

Protective styling | Wild child

Natural products | Whatever gets the job done

Homemade | Store bought

Tender-headed | Hurt me so good

Sweat it out | Tie it down

Highlights | Color me bad

THE LONG AND SHORT OF IT

Subtle | Bold

Precision cut | Subtle cascade

My texture | Someone else's texture

Product junkie | Tried and true

Hair shows | No go's

Shaved hair line | Natural hair line

Salt and pepper | Dye to hide the gray

Trendsetter | Trend follower

Silk cap | Silk pillowcase

Blow dry | Air dry

Product swaps | Brand new

Wash and go | Set it, then forget it

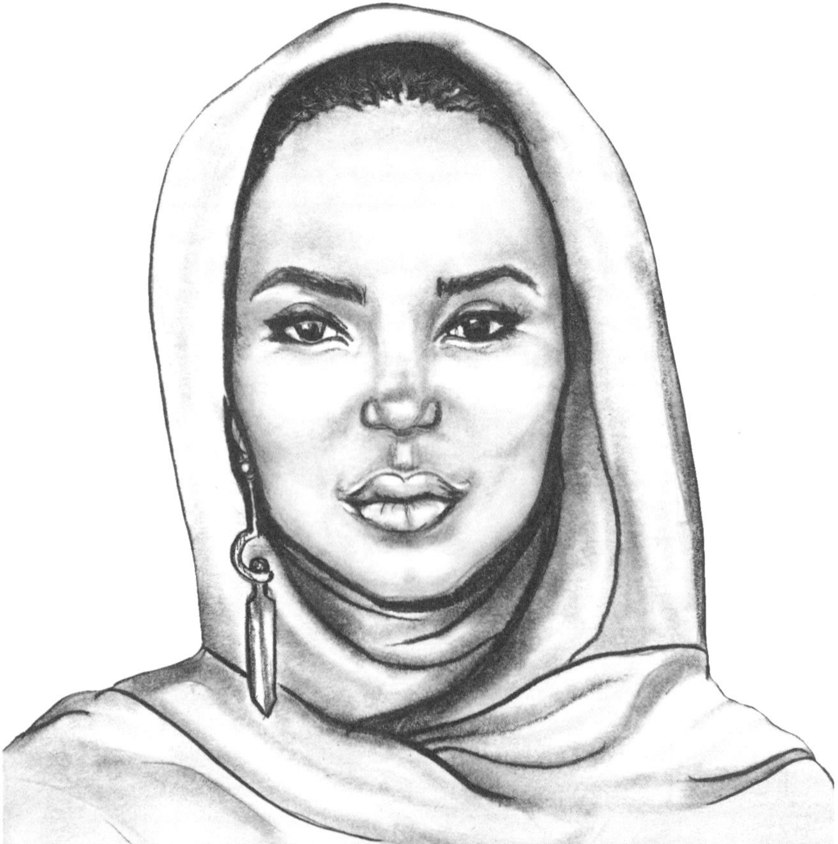

Curl Connection

Hair is a
- ○ Bridge
- ○ Wall
- ○ Both a bridge and a wall

between people.

I influenced the following people to go natural:

The person who said they would never go natural and did:

The person who said they would never go natural and still hasn't:

CURL CONNECTION

The first time my family saw my all natural hair:

The first time my co-workers saw my all natural hair:

The person who always compliments my hair:

The person who always makes me feel badly about my natural hair:

CURL CONNECTION

The person who has tried to copy my haircut or style:

The person whose haircut or style I have copied:

The person who feels comfortable touching my natural hair without asking:

I have touched people's hair without asking: ◯ Yes or ◯ No

A stranger has touched my hair without permission: ◯ Yes or ◯ No

  If yes, how did you respond?

The question about my hair that I find most annoying and/or offensive:

CURL CONNECTION

The question about my hair that I most enjoy answering:

3 common assumptions people make about natural hair:

　　1)

　　2)

　　3)

I am familiar with the hair plight of other cultures: ○ Yes or ○ No

I am familiar with natural hair styling internationally: ○ Yes or ○ No

A person who always talks about her hair:

CURL CONNECTION

Is there such thing as a natural hair snob: ○ Yes or ○ No

If yes, what are the characteristics of such a person:

I freely share things about my hair: ○ Yes or ○ No

I prefer to keep my styling tips, products, and techniques to myself: ○ Yes or ○ No

Something I do to my hair that I don't want other people to know about?

Natural Hair Tool Kit

Build a Natural Hair Toolkit

What are your absolute must have products, tools, and resources for going natural? List or sketch them here. Give your toolkit to a friend thinking about or in the beginning stages of going natural.

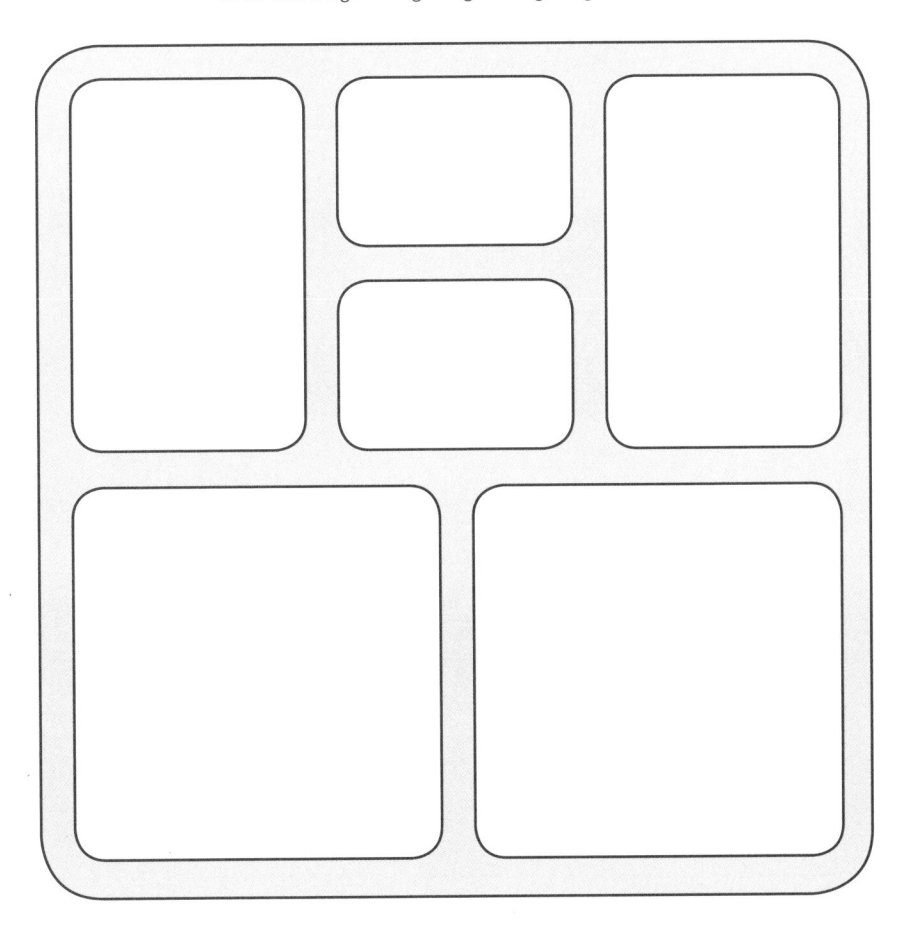

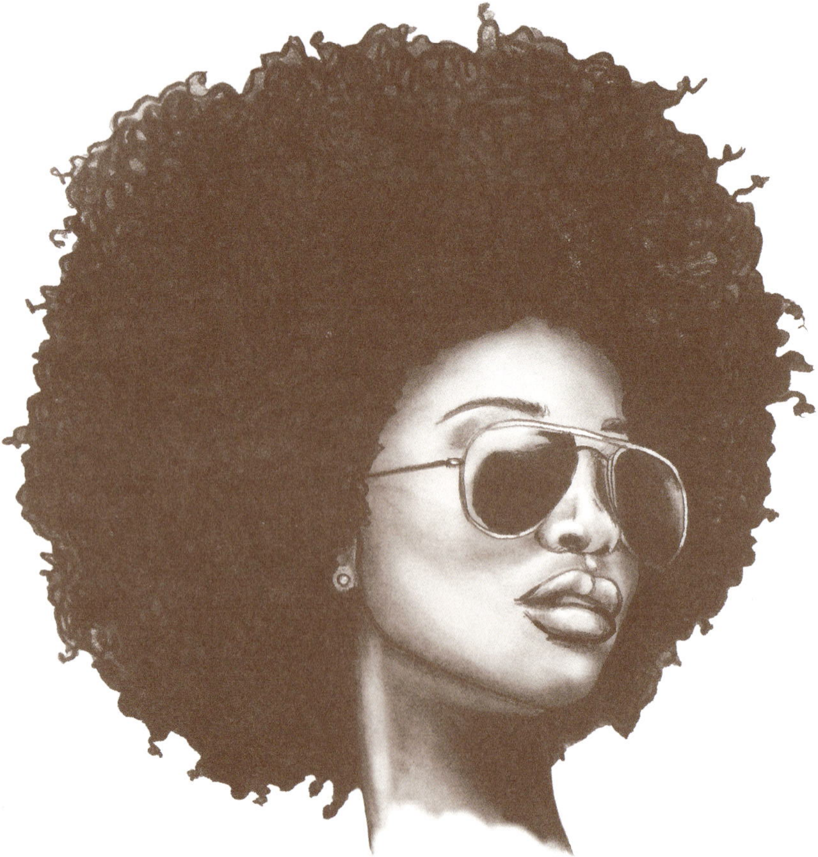

Media Frizz

Natural hair is adequately represented in the mainstream media: ○ *True* or ○ *False*

The media influences how I feel about my hair: ○ *Yes* or ○ *No*

If yes, how?

MEDIA FRIZZ

Celebrities have an influence on how I feel about my hair: ○ Yes or ○ No

Why or why not?

How?

The last natural style I saw on a movie, TV show, or commercial was:

The Afro image is the best symbol to represent natural hair: ○ True or ○ False

MEDIA FRIZZ

The symbol I would use to represent natural hair:

The number of books I have read on the subject of natural hair:

The number of videos I have watched on the subject of natural hair:

The number of articles I have read on the subject of natural hair:

If I could talk to anyone in the world about their hair, I would speak to:

The first question I would ask her or him:

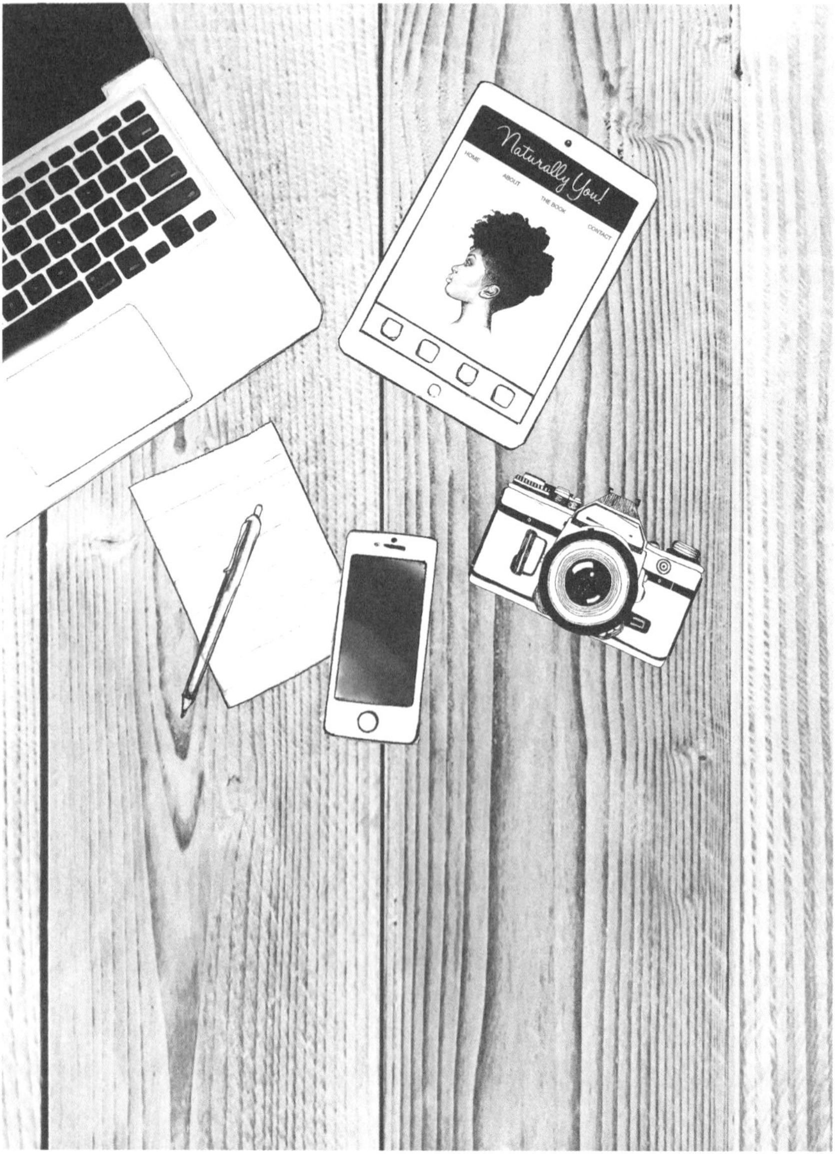
Naturally You!
HOME
ABOUT
THE BOOK
CONTACT

Blogs and Vlogs and Posts, Oh My!

The social medium I use the most as it relates to natural hair:
- ○ Facebook
- ○ YouTube
- ○ Pinterest
- ○ Tumblr
- ○ Instagram
- ○ Other:

The number of sites related to natural hair I visit in a week:

I spend too much time online as it relates to natural hair: ○ Yes or ○ No

The name I go by online:

I have used social media to create a natural hair community for myself: ○ Yes or ○ No

BLOGS, VLOGS AND POSTS, OH MY!

The groups I follow on social media:

I rely on the opinions and reviews of bloggers and/or vloggers: ○ Yes or ○ No

Bloggers I follow:

Vloggers I follow:

What I like most about natural hair bloggers/vloggers:

BLOGS, VLOGS AND POSTS, OH MY!

What I like least about hair bloggers/vloggers:

Bloggers/vloggers should be compensated for product reviews: ○ Yes or ○ No

Compensation influences the credibility of a blogger/vlogger: ○ Yes or ○ No

I only follow people that have my same hair type: ○ Yes or ○ No

I've posted pictures of my hair online: ○ Yes or ○ No

I've posted a natural hair video tutorial online: ○ Yes or ○ No

I have written a review of a service, product, business: ○ Yes or ○ No

If I created a blog/vlog about natural hair, it would focus on:

BLOGS, VLOGS AND POSTS, OH MY!

The name of my blog/vlog would be:

I am a regular blogger: ○ Yes or ○ No

I am a regular vlogger: ○ Yes or ○ No

I have received free product(s) from a hair product company: ○ Yes or ○ No

My favorite natural hair saying or meme:

The funniest natural hair meme:

Social Media Ready

BEGINNER Challenge: Write a product review and submit it to your favorite blog site.

INTERMEDIATE Challenge: Create a 10-minute instructional video of your favorite style and post it online.

ADVANCED Challenge for the professional blogger/vlogger: Write an editorial and submit it to your favorite magazine for publishing.

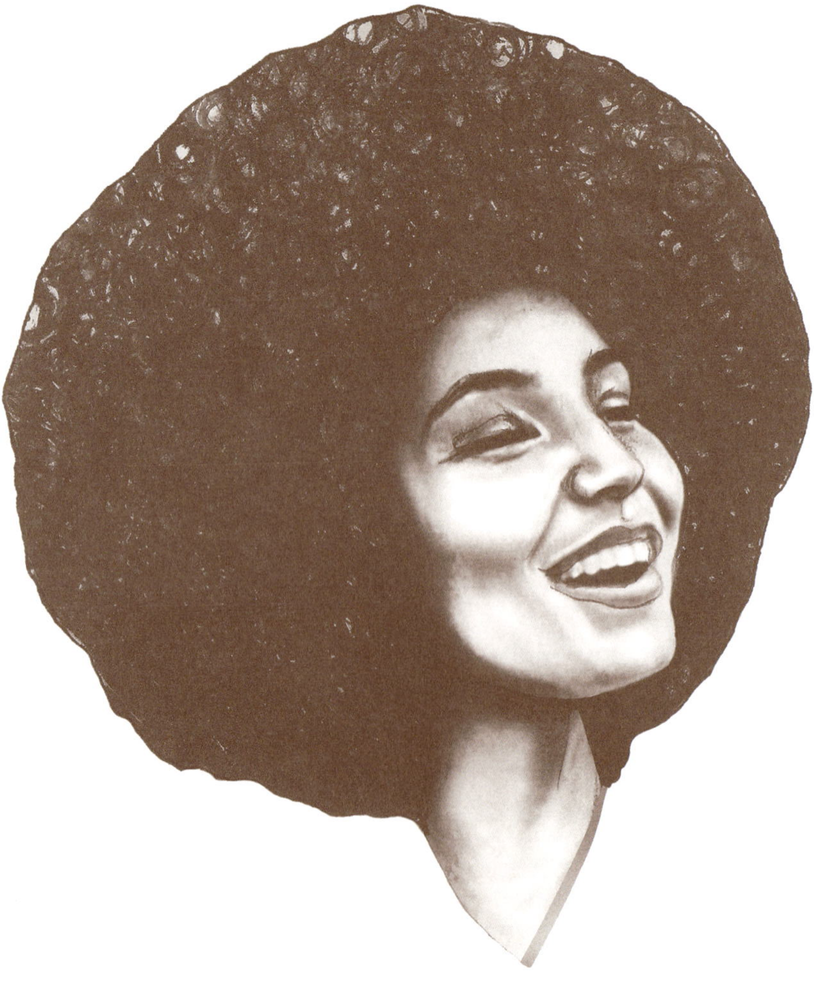

The Hall of Mane Fame

My favorite natural hair...

Corporate Style

Vintage Style

Protective Style

Winter/Fall Do

Summer/Spring Do

Stylist

THE HALL OF MANE FAME

Blogger

Vlogger

Website/Blog

Magazine

Book

Children's Book

Trade Show

Length

Tool

THE HALL OF MANE FAME

Shampoo

Conditioner

Moisturizer

Holding product

Celebrity

Accessory

Product Scent

Store to buy products/tools

Paraphernalia

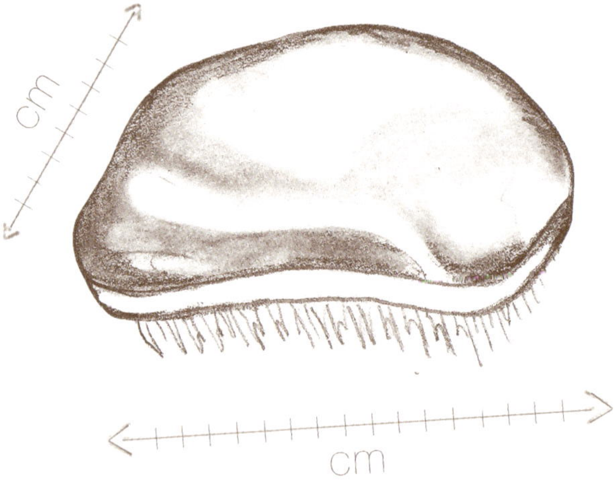
cm
cm

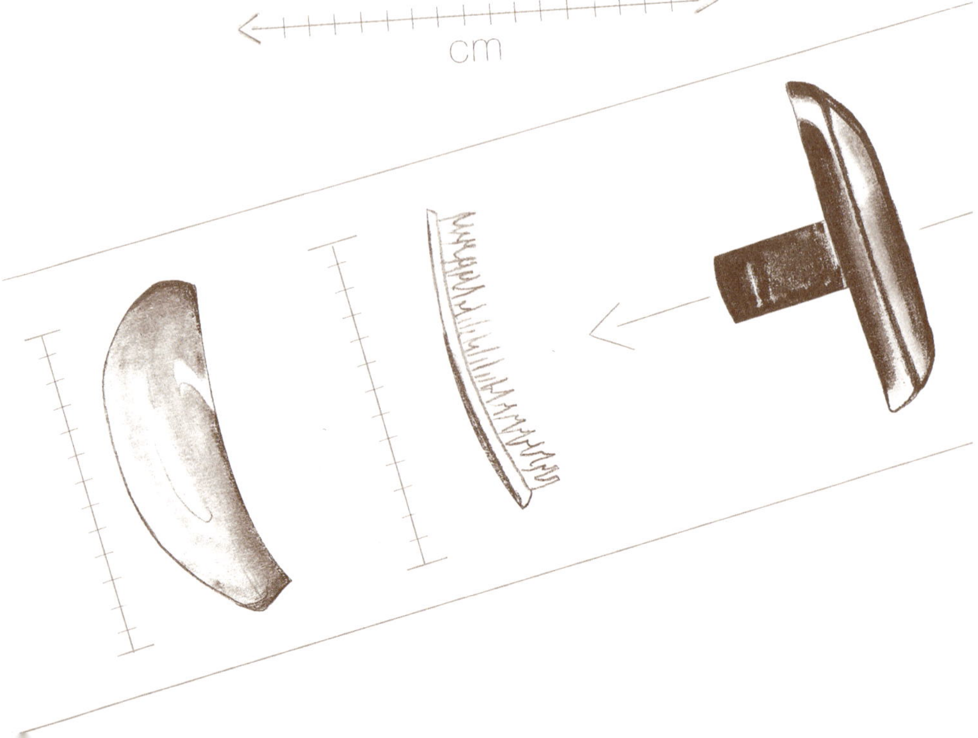

Hair Innovation

What product or tool is missing from the natural hair market?

Have an idea?

Name

Description

HAIR INNOVATION

Recipe/materials

Target market

Target price

Competition

Where will it sell?

Hair Innovation: Sketch Pad

Hair Innovation: Sketch Pad

Hair Innovation: Sketch Pad

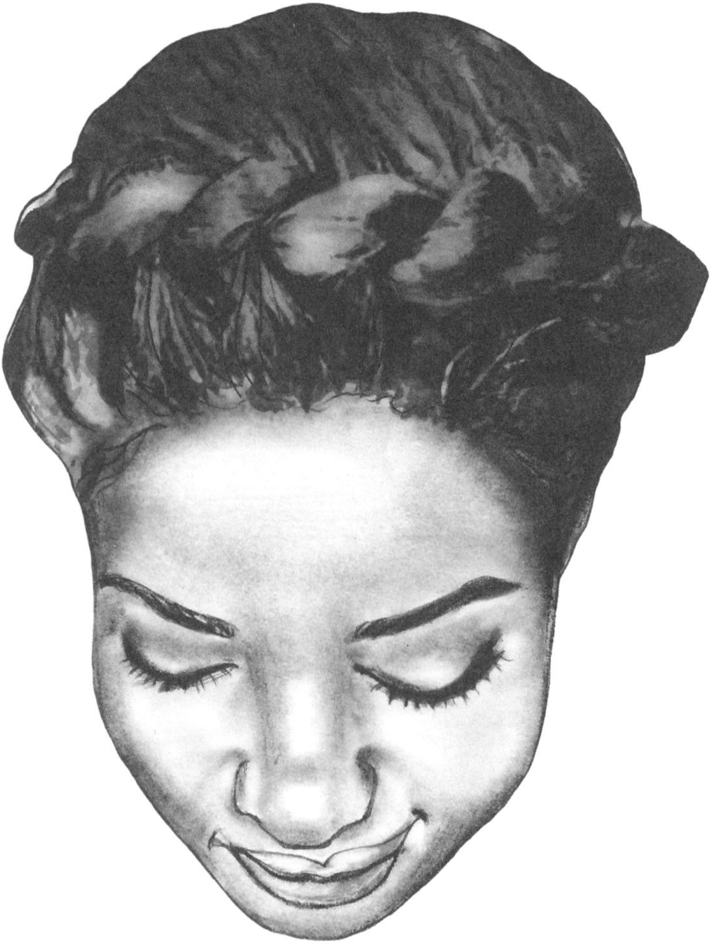

Natural Hair Glossary of Terms

There are a lot of words specific to the natural hair movement. Use the blank pages to add other words as you come across them.

BC – Big Chop: the process of cutting off the relaxed or permed ends of one's hair when transitioning from chemically processed hair to natural hair.

Curly: hair pattern where the strands form a continuous s-shape ranging from loose to tighter spirals.

Co-Wash: a method of cleansing your hair with conditioner instead of shampoo.

Creamy crack: a term that defines a straightening relaxer. Due to its need to be consistently reapplied a relaxer is sometimes viewed as an addictive product. The term is considered by some to be derogatory.

Kinky: hair pattern where the strands turn in on themselves creating a tightly coiled, zigzag or z-pattern.

Protective hairstyle: a hair style that keeps hair ends tucked away from everyday exposure to the elements; sun, rain, wind, etc.

Transitioning: the gradual steps of going from chemically processed to natural hair; usually involves growing one's hair out while trimming the ends a little at a time.

TWA - Teeny Weeny Afro: A small Afro about 1/2 - 1 inch of hair in length.

GLOSSARY

GLOSSARY

GLOSSARY

Free Style Flow aka Notes

Use this space for additional journaling.

FREE STYLE FLOW

FREE STYLE FLOW

FREE STYLE FLOW

FREE STYLE FLOW

FREE STYLE FLOW

FREE STYLE FLOW

FREE STYLE FLOW

Acknowledgements

I am immensely grateful for all of the naturalistas and naturalista supporters. Hair that inspires life is truly a blessing.

A very special thank you to a team of talented and dynamic contributors:

Editor, Cherise Fisher of The Scribes Window
Illustrator, Philece R.
Designer, Brian Hodge

Thank you to my family and dear friends whose favorite pastime is great conversation.

Lots of love to my husband and children who make life dynamic and beautiful.